A MOSAIC

Freemasonry and the Art of Memory

Martin Faulks

Lewis Masonic

To Kindra Jones,
who has been my corporeal similitude of academic rigour

First published 2018

ISBN 978 0 85318 562 8

© Martin Faulks 2018
Edited by Kindra Jones

Published by Lewis Masonic

an imprint of Ian Allan Publishing Ltd, Addlestone, Surrey KT15 2SF.
Printed in England.

Visit the Lewis Masonic website at www.lewismasonic.co.uk

'The Warden of the Lodge. . . shall take trial of the art of memory and science thereof of every fellow craft and every apprentice according to their vocation and in case that they have lost any point thereof. . . pay the penalty as follows for their slothfulness. . .' Second Schaw Statutes of 1599.

'The Schaw Statutes' is a document of great importance to Masonic history as it laid the foundations for organised lodges. Issued by the then royally appointed Master of the Works, William Schaw, the text gave a set of rules designed to govern the activities of operative masons in Scotland at the turn of the seventeenth century. His second edition of the Statutes written in 1599, and from which the above quote was drawn, addressed the issue of the local organisation of lodges and gave the Lodge of Kilwinning (No. 0, GL of Scotland) supervisory powers over the lodges of west Scotland. The second statutes is often seen by some as a 'prototype' of those regulations which now govern the provincial structure of Freemasonry. Both statutes were preserved in ancient Scottish lodges showing that they were most certainly taken seriously at the time. Indeed, the Aitchison's Haven Lodge in Edinburgh owned a copy showing updates made in 1661 when new rules were added by the lodge,[1] demonstrating its use as a rule book to govern the lodge and the Masons in it.

Upon first reading of the art of memory within the Schaw Statutes, a common misunderstanding is to assume it is a reference to simply retaining knowledge as needed by an operative mason or builder. However, if the whole text is studied it soon becomes apparent that this is likely to be incorrect since the skills and knowledge pertaining to the practical training of the stonemason is covered earlier on in the document. Indeed, to contemporary society the specific phrase 'art of memory'[2] had far greater connotations than it may to the modern

[1] Stephenson, D., *The Origins of Freemasonry* (Cambridge University Press, 1990) 44
[2] *Oratoriae Artis Epitomata*, a work by Jacobus Publicius printed at Venice in 1482, is apparently the first to mention *memoriae ars*. For an earlier use of *ars memorie artificialis* in a 14th century. Italian source see F. A. Yates *Art of Memory* (1966) iv. 90

reader. In early modern correspondence and publications it would seem that this term was always used specifically to refer to a specific set of memory disciplines and techniques that had evolved from classical Greek mnemonics.[3]

The modus operandi of mnemonics normally involved the imaginative reconstruction of a building called a 'memory palace' in which key personalities, items or symbols were placed at distinct points as prompts for whatever it was the practitioner wanted to recall. By the sixteenth century the art of memory had a strong tradition in the British Isles, having been very much a part of medieval culture, and was seeing a resurgence in popularity during the the Renaissance with new and varied forms very much in vogue. Indeed from 1500 to 1699 over 350 books were published either on or mentioning the art of memory, with a peak in popularity appearing in 1640 which saw over 68 books making mention of the art.[4]

Returning to the Statutes, the context of the duty to practice the art of memory seems to be more focused on lodge membership as it comes after all the rules involving practical matters and the qualifications for becoming a member. There are strong hints in the first Schaw Statutes of some form of initiation or 'entering' ceremony. Although there is no evidence of the exact entering ceremony of the time, as the 'Mason Craft' spread over the next hundred years more gentlemen Masons were admitted and fragments of rituals from this time show something of what was taking place. The content of these catechistic memory tests[5] largely matches with what is practiced in modern day Freemasonry.[6]

From the earliest exposés of Freemasonry it can be seen that prior to the construction of physical lodge buildings the ceremonies were

[3] For a full assessment of the term 'art of memory' at this time see William E Engel's, *The Memory Arts in Renaissance England*: A Critical Anthology (Cambridge University Press 2016) Also see Fabio Venzi's *Studies on Traditional Freemasonry* (Lewis Masonic 2013)
[4] English Books Online Database Search
[5] Douglas. Jones, G. P. Hamer, Douglas. Carr, Harry Knoop, *Early Masonic Catechisms* (1963)
[6] Robert Kirk, *The Secret Commonwealth (Commonwealth) & A Short Treatise of Charms and Spels* 1691 See the appendix for the first evidence of the use of the passwords, signs and tokens.

based around an imaginary recreation of Solomon's Temple, with symbolic images drawn on the floor of a tavern to aid the imagination and with specific officers placed in different positions in the lodge. A memory palace of sorts? It's also worth noting at this point that Francis Yates, an eminent expert on mnemonics, upon seeing modern Masonic ritual instantly identified it as a form of the art of memory without knowing anything of Schaw and his statutes.[7]

With the great focus Freemasonry has placed since earliest times on memory, and evidence of a ritual system appearing from various sources soon after the Schaw Statutes, it seems logical to conclude that the art of memory Schaw was referring to was an early form of Masonic ritual. So, if Masonic ritual was seen by Schaw as a form of the art of memory, and it seems so to modern memory experts, then which memory school was it part of? Just as martial arts have many styles and traditions, so too does the art of memory.

Some have concluded that this was a reference to what could be called the mystical Hermetic art of memory, as popularised by Giordano Bruno and Robert Fludd, and that this was something that Schaw was introducing into the lodges.[8] This could seem like a reasonable conclusion when looking at what was happening in Scotland at the time. The court of James VI was indeed a place where the Hermetic art of memory flourished, and at least two of the Schaw's associates there were experts in the art.

Often it is suggested that the proximity of Schaw to Alexander Dicsone, Giordano Bruno's personal student,[9] in the Scottish Court could explain the Masonic link to the art of memory and specifically the Hermetic style. In fact, Dicsone even featured in Bruno's works and produced a book outlining his own Hermetic memory system

---

[7] Dame Frances Yates, *The Art of Memory* (Routledge & Kegan Paul 1966) 303-306

[8] Professor David Stephenson *The Origins of Freemasonry* (Cambridge University Press 1990) See for the most detailed case for this. Likewise Robert Cooper in his *Cracking the Freemason's Code (5 Oct 2006)* supports this view to some degree.

[9] In his *Cena de le Censeri (London,1584)* Bruno speaks of 'that clever, honest, kind, gentlemanly and faithful friend, Alexander Dickson,' and indeed makes 'Dicsono' a speaker in one of the dialogues in the collection, De la Causa.

inspired by Bruno's teachings.[10] Likewise William Fowler, another member of court, was a memory master. Fowler studied the classical art of memory and worked as Secretary to the Queen of Denmark. He was well known for his memory arts and even taught the art of memory to the King himself. In return for being taught poetry.[11] There is evidence that as time went on Masons were seen as almost mythical figures in Scotland, and even came to be associated with Rosicrucianism. Indeed the 'Masons' Word' itself was said to be able to grant magical powers.[12] All this could seems to point at the Hermetic art of memory, but could there be another explanation?

England and Scotland had an early tradition of memory arts and by the time of Schaw these methods were widespread throughout. Indeed the first memory manual in English was published in 1333,[13] so Bruno's art was by no means a new introduction. Just because associates of Schaw practiced the then popular Hermetic art of memory does not mean this was the art he was recommending, even if Schaw himself was a practitioner. After all, it's possible for a pianist to encourage the study of a musical instrument without specifically meaning the piano. Likewise the view many people have of Freemasonry modernly is conclusive proof that the attitude of the general public should not be relied upon for an accurate view of the Craft, since if popular conspiracy theories were believed by future historians, then they would have to conclude that Masons secretly controlled the world in the twenty-first century.

It has been suggested that given the Scottish pride of tradition (which is very present in the Statutes themselves) it would seem rather implausible that anyone could introduce a new tradition of ritual memory into an already up and running Scottish lodge tradition. Perhaps rather than introducing a new form of Hermetic spirituality

---

[10] Alexander Dicksone, *De Umbra Rationis et Iudicii* (1584)

[11] *Works of William Fowler* (Scottish Text Society Productions 1940) , vol 3 35

[12] Jones, G. P. Hamer, Douglas. Carr, Harry Knoop *Early Masonic Catechisms*. (Manchester University Press 1963)

[13] Thomas Bradwardine, *De Memoria Artificiale 1321*, trans. M. Carruthers (in 'The Journal of Medieval Latin', 2, 1992)

into the stonemason lodges, Schaw was referring to a pre-existing tradition in the lodge that involved memory. There was an ubiquitous Christian mnemonic tradition prevalent in the culture at the time and, considering the very close association that the lodges had with the Church,[14] it is entirely possible that this was the tradition Schaw was referring to. There is even evidence that some of the most early speculative Masons were clergymen and that the Church had some say over appointments in the lodge. Schaw was a Catholic and, considering the sensitive religious climate of the time, he had needed to learn to be careful. Perhaps he thought it more tactful, and indeed safe, in his constitutions to use the term 'art of memory' rather than something such as 'Ancient Secret Initiation Ceremonies'.

Is it possible that the notorious has been mistaken for the likely? Could some authorities be too quick in associating Freemasonry with the Hermetic art of memory?

So which art of memory was it? Rather than rely of circumstantial evidence like who Schaw knew, or how Freemasonry was viewed, it should be possible to explore the various schools of mnemonics and compare their methods of memorisation to Masonic tradition. Unlike in other areas of study where it is often very difficult to pick up threads hundreds of years old, there are two distinct advantages in using this approach in this situation. Firstly, because mnemonic techniques are specifically designed to be memorable they are very persistent, surviving in the group consciousness even when words and cultures change, and as empires rise and fall. Secondly, although Masonic rituals may been elaborated on over the years, and lodges opened and closed, the love of tradition within the Masonic world and the protection offered by a continuous current to the present day, means that if the origins of Freemasonry's rituals really are a product of the art of memory, then the methods of a recognisable mnemonic system should be imprinted upon the Craft and clear for those with the eyes to see.

---

[14] The *Schaw Statutes* themselves clearly state 'the wardens of every lodge shall be answerable to the Presbytries [courts of the church].'

Remembering Schools of Memory

As a race humanity has naturally found methods to make things more memorable; the use of rhyme in poems, the storing of information in dramatic stories, and songs have all helped information to stick in the mind and ensure the passing of knowledge down the generations. Everyone knows a few of these simple mnemonic practices, with some even being employed within schools, whether it's the popular method of using acronyms (like using the sentence 'Richard Of York Gave Battle In Vain' to remember the colours of the rainbow); imagining a funny or exciting image; or an association with an action, such as the simple act of tying a knot in a handkerchief.

Memory was of course far more important in ancient times before writing, and subsequently printing, became prevalent. As such most societies had specialists who were given the task of storing key knowledge and developed methods beyond that practised by general society: in India the Brahman, in the British Isles (as Tacitus reports) the druids, and in pre-Socratic Greece the orators. These memory specialists tended to develop more advanced methods of artificial memory in order to practice their art, and it is from these Greek orators in antiquity that the oldest known memory system has been inherited, which tends to be referred to as the classical art of memory. It is from this tradition that all the other schools of the art of memory evolved. This paper will be covering the three main schools of memory - the classical, the Christian, and the Hermetic. It's important to note there were other schools, some which were very mystical and idiosyncratic, and others very dry and logical, but these either post-date the Schaw Statutes, or were far less influential, not having the patronage of courtiers or the backing of the Church. As such none had the same momentum to influence the Craft to any degree.

Whilst considering these artificial memory systems, it's worth noting that these methods tended to become part of the culture and started to be used in some form as an unconscious part of any learning. So just as in the modern day people tend to number a list of things to recall as an aide-mémoire, so too did people use the memory methods of their day without necessarily being aware they were doing such.

The Classical Art of Memory

The traditional story of the discovery of the art of memory was told by Cicero in his book *On Oratory*, which attributes its creation to a famous pre-Socratic poet called Simonides of Ceos.[15] The story goes as follows:

Simonides of Ceos was a great poet who was employed to recite an ode at the banquet of a nobleman. He began by dedicating the poem to both his host and the twin stars, Castor and Pollux. The speech was breathtakingly beautiful and pleased all who heard it. However, when it was completed his employer objected, arguing that he should only have to pay half of Simonides' fee. Since half of the poem was dedicated to the twin stars, they could pay him for the rest. Within minutes the meal was disturbed when a message was brought to Simonides informing him that two young men were waiting at the

door of the house and wished to talk to him. He left to see who was there, but no one was waiting. In that moment the banquet hall collapsed, killing the nobleman, his family, and all the dinner guests.

Castor and Pollux, the twin heavenly brothers, had indeed paid their half of the fee! However, the rewards for Simonides had not ended.

As the rubble was removed the poor victims of the collapse were found to be so mangled that they could not be recognised, even by their own families. Simonides, who wanted to help them mourn and bury their dead, found that, to his surprise, he could recall a perfect image of the banqueting hall including the exact

---

[15] Simonides of Ceos (556 – 468 BC) was a Greek lyric poet, born at Ioulis on Ceos.

locations of the guests at the table relative to each other, what they were eating, and who they had talked to.

From this amazing experience Simonides proceeded to create the first classical example of the art of memory. In a sense, the first memory palace had been discovered!

Symbolically the art of memory being inspired by twins has great meaning as in a sense memory is the art of making an exact copy of something, just as one twin is a copy of the other. The tale of Simonides' disastrous feast beautifully illustrates the rules of the art of memory whereby an imaginary scene is used to place things the practitioner wishes to remember in specific emotive and memorable locations. The rules for this method later became formalised in rhetorical manuals, some of which have survived to the present day.

For the purpose of this ongoing inquiry it is vital the reader gain a clear understanding of the methods of this memory art, and how better to do this than by utilising an ancient treatise on the subject. Thus here is summarised the method taught in the anonymously written but hugely influential classical text *Ad Herennium* from *c.*80 BC.

The Method of the Art of Memory Summarised
The first step in the art of memory is to create a memory palace. This is an imaginary backdrop to be used for future memory work. Once the memory palace has been created in the practitioner's mind, they are then able to revisit whenever they wish, to place whatever it is they wish to remember there. Thus the practitioner should then be able to return to their memory palace to recall with ease.

How to Make a Memory Palace
1) Choose a building or location which is exciting, inspiring, and small enough to easily remember. Some good examples of this would be a house, a room with many columns, a recess, an arch, or even a picture can be used.
2) Visualise walking around this place in the imagination, stopping at specific locations in turn. Each stop in this imaginary tour should have something of interest in it. A good example would

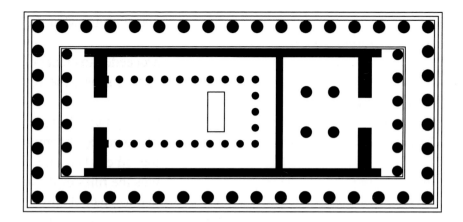

be a statue, mark, portrait, or object that holds a strong like or dislike. The position for each station or location should be very different and well spaced out (about 30 feet apart is ideal). A number or letter can also be associated with each place.

3) Practice walking the memory palace repeatedly using the imagination to its full potential, ensuring all the senses are engaged until the palace can be walked through with ease, always keeping to the same route and stopping at the same places of interest.

If a real place is used as the memory palace it's best to choose somewhere which is quiet, with few people present, and not too bright or dark, so the mind is not distracted whilst walking from station to station. This allows the locations to be imprinted with ease. Whilst walking through the palace study with special care each location adopted so that they may cling lastingly in the memory. This is important as these set stations in the memory palace act as the filing system for future memorisation.

Consider this newly formed memory palace as a wax tablet or notebook, ready to be used to record anything that needs to be remembered. This practice can also be elaborated if needed by forming different themed memory palaces to store information on specific subjects. However, it's important to make sure that each palace is distinct and very different from one another.

Once the memory palace is created it is time to practice adding the things to remember.

Adding Images

To add images to the memory palace the practitioner must walk through and stop at each of the set locations to place the images representing the things to remember in order. The images should be exciting, unusual, horrifying, amusing, or otherwise strongly emotional and stimulating so as to be easy to recall. Use images that are connected with the subject matter and if possible find a memorable way of connecting the memory image with the location. So, for example, if the item to be remembered is bravery and its location in the palace is the bathroom, perhaps imagine a lion taking a bath; for vigilance an eagle on a hatstand; or for humour a clown falling down the stairs will really stand out. Use puns, double entendres, references from popular culture, and creatively linked ideas to make sure that there is the detail and specifics to trigger the memory.

Remembering Words

The method already outlined is a wonderful tool for remembering objects and lists, but it can also be used to remember words. If trying to remember a section of text images can be placed that contain triggers for the words in the correct place instead. Further detail can be added by having the image contain specifics that will help to remember particular information due in the talk. For example, if wanting to remember a speech that describes a life story involving many different people, imagine each key person as a figure in each location in the order they appear in the speech. To add extra information add greater detail to the figure, such as specific clothing or giving them objects to hold that will trigger points to be made or represent key events. Use creativity to link the image to the speech in a way that will stand out and so be memorable. With practice an experienced practitioner can encompass the record of an entire matter in a single image.

These are the rules of the classical form of the art of memory as said to be invented by Simonides. It may of course be that there is no truth to this story, but from references in Cicero, Quintilianus, Pliny, Aelian, Suidas, and many more it is clear that he is universally seen as the creator of mnemonics.

Historical Evidence

In addition to some hints and subtle references to the art of memory in pre-Socratic philosophical texts, there survives a direct instructional text that conclusively proves that the memory arts were developing about the time the legend of Simonides claims. The apparently Sophist fragment known as the *Dissoi Logoi* (opposing arguments) is dated to *c.*400 BC and contains a tiny section on memory:

> 'The greatest and fairest discovery has been found to be memory; it is useful for everything, for wisdom as well as for the conduct of life. This is the first step: if you focus your attention, your mind, making progress by this means, will perceive more. The second step is to practice whatever you hear. If you hear the same things many times and repeat them, what you have learned presents itself to your memory as a connected whole. The third step is: whenever you hear something, connect it with what you know already. For instance, suppose you need to remember the name 'Chrysippos', you must connect it with *chrusos* (gold) and *hippos* (horse). Or another example: if you need to remember the name 'Pyrilampes' you must connect it with pyr (fire) and lampein (to shine). These are examples for words. In the case of things, do this: if you want to remember courage, think of Ares and Achilles.'[16]

[16] Sprague, R. 'Dissoi Logoi or Dialexeis' *Mind* - Vol. 77 No. 306 (April, 1968) 155-167 166-167

This primitive outline of the rules of artificial memory from about fifty years after the death of Simonides contains a clear but basic description of methods which are recorded later on in more detailed works. This practice, as noted above, of connecting the notion or word to be remembered with a dramatic image recurs all through the history of the art of memory, as does the use of plays on words and rhyming.

Some scholars of mnemonic works have noted that the specific way of using Greek terminology in *Dissoi Logoi* would become the norm in later mnemonic works and that this is the first known example of the traditional division of memory practices into memory for things and memory for words (or in this case names).[17] All that was missing was the rules for places. Also please notice the association between memory and morality, with a suggestion the character can be improved through the practice of memorisation of virtues and vices. This will become far more important further on.

As time went on the art of memory developed and evolved. The method always involved a building or physical location of some type, normally of an emotive, religious, or easy to remember nature, with a series of different colourful characters or people standing in set, easy to remember places that could be visited in order. With daily practice a practitioner of this art could build up the image of a temple or place in their imagination so clearly that it was as if they were walking there in reality. Facts to be remembered were represented by objects or personalities placed in set locations on the way. When the practitioner then wanted to recall a list, or a very long text, they could with minimal mental effort simply revisit the memory palace and see the objects in order in their set locations. It was if they had simply remained where they had been placed previously.

This art was also used more subtly in ancient Greek works, such as in speeches that deliberately took the audience on a journey with very important and powerful points tied to different locations. Philosophical texts were often written in an interlocutory style, a

---

[17] Frances Yates, *The Art of Memory* (Routledge & Kegan Paul 1966) 30

format that was easy to remember, and with different people bringing up different subjects in memorable varied locations. All of Plato's outstanding works were written to this format. It is also known that philosophers made a practice of memorising lengthy discourses that had been created in this manner.

Aristotle not only mentioned the art of memory many times in his works,[18] but he also outlined mnemonic methods in his books. He went so far as to suggest the true philosopher should practice the art of memory, but stressed that this was not some form of mystical practice or meditation, but rather for practical purposes, the goal being to be able to memorise common objections to an argument in order to prepare properly for debates.[19] In this Aristotle's approach was standard for the time, since the classical art of memory was almost always represented as part of the art of speaking and purely utilitarian, the methods used were whatever worked. If it stood out in the mind, it was included. Furthermore, it is thought that Aristotle may have written his own work on mnemonics[20] that is now lost. With Aristotle's school of philosophy being known as the Peripatetic school due to the practice they had of walking during lessons and discussions, it's tempting to think that they could have been using the art of memory in a very direct way, perhaps moving from topic to topic as they walked in the Lyceum,[21] using it as a memory temple.

For the philosophers the memory was something divine. The ability to make an imprint in the mind was a demonstration of the higher nature of man. The memorisation of truth, the speaking of truth, and living that truth was all part of the philosopher's path. The practical applications of this art meant that this method of memorisation became widely spread in ancient western civilisation with many politicians, public speakers, and perhaps most of all solicitors learning the art. The Romans continued to develop the skill

[18] I have found mentions of this art in *De anima*, *Topics* and of course *On Memory and Recollection*
[19] Aristotle – *Topics*
[20] Diogenes Laertius, *Lives of the Philosophers*, Life of Aristotle, (Loeb Classical Library 1925), V. 26.
[21] A garden in Athens with covered walks where Aristotle taught his philosophy.

and it was said that some public speakers took their ability to such extreme levels that they were able to memorise the names of every villager before they visited to give a talk.

However, there are hints that even in ancient times some practiced the art of memory in a more mystical manner. Some writers clearly connect mnemonics with the magical 'Chaldæan arts.'[22] Memory-training for religious purposes was prominent in the revival of Pythagoreanism and the Neoplatonic lineage in late antiquity. Iamblichus, Porphyry, and Diogenes believed Pythagoras was a expert in memory and Philostratus even mentioned Simonides in his account of the mystical memory arts of the Neopythagorean Apollonius of Tyana.[23] It's also often repeated that the fifth century philosopher Metrodorus of Lampsacus used the signs of the zodiac and the decans as his memory palace, but this was certainly an exception with most practitioners using their home or public place. However, this exception may hint at a more spiritual approach and the beginnings of a change of direction for the art of memory.

With the fall of the Roman Empire much knowledge was lost, but the art of memory had the inherent advantage of being designed specifically to remain firm in the minds of men. Not only that, but it also survived in the form of instruction manuals and in language,[24] waiting like a phoenix to rise again in a new form.

---

[22] Philostratus and Eunapius, *The Lives of the Sophists* (Life of Dionysius of Miletus), trans. W. C. Wright, (Loeb Classical Library 1925), 91-93.
[23] Philostratus, *Life of Apollonius of Tyana*, I, 14; trans. C. P. Halls (Stanford University Press, 1923) 15.
[24] The word 'topic' comes from the Latin *topica*, which in turn derives from the Greek *ta topika* meaning place or location, and is thought to evolve from the use of place in the art of memory to remember a subject to talk about about.

The Christian Craft of Memory

As Rome fell many people were slain, including one of the first known Christian memory masters, the man known as St Augustine. A renowned expert in rhetoric, from reading his *Confessions* it can be seen that he used mnemonics[25] as a practical aid to his studies. St Augustine believed the holy trinity of God was reflected in man; the father being the soul, the memory the son, and the will the holy ghost.[26] To the saint the memory was thus something divine in man, an ability to recreate things inside that, although a shadow of the creative power of the Lord himself, if used correctly could help one follow the narrow path of salvation as laid out in the biblical texts.

Rome had fallen, but records of its education system remained in the realms of Christendom and over time 'lost' knowledge was rediscovered. With Cicero's works as core source material, education started to blossom, but in a new form. Gone were the interlocutory style texts, replaced with catechistical learning methods and writings. The seven classical liberal arts of the Romans were made a focus, backed by biblical support:

'Wisdom hath builded her house, she hath hewn out her seven pillars:' (Proverbs 9:1)

Additionally the classical virtues of temperance, fortitude, prudence, and justice[27] supplied in Roman texts were added to the three spiritual virtues of faith, hope, and charity found in the Bible, creating a beautiful symmetry. In the thirteenth century the Dominican monks St Albert the Great and his pupil, St Thomas Aquinas, took the fore and the principles of memory were once again fully taken on board and incorporated into learning, this time with a new flair. At the time the *Rhetorica Ad Herennium* was thought to be by Cicero, or 'Tullius' as they called him, and the rules were taken as law. However, although previously the art of memory had been used to aid

---

[25] Saint Augustine *Confessions*, (Pocket Books, 1907) X, 8.
[26] Saint Augustine *De Trinitate*, (Cambridge University Press, 2002) IX, 6, xi.
[27] Corresponding to the four classical elements as follows Temperance - Air, Fortitude - Earth, Prudence - water, Justice - Fire

recollection, St Albert and St Thomas started to move memory into the realm of ethics.

Unsurprisingly during this time biblical imagery and locations became the most popular form of memory palaces. Indeed there are detailed instruction manuals using biblical temples, noah's ark (using the animals as locations),[28] the coat of many colours, Jacob's ladder, Aaron's breastplate (using the jewels),[29] King Solomon's temple,[30] and even the wings of an angel was used as a memory palace.[31] Of course actual physical locations that could be visited were generally considered to make the best memory palaces and so churches became much favoured. The churches lent themselves well to this art, having saints and biblical figures at fixed locations around the building, giving the practitioner easy points for their inner pilgrimage. So popular was this art, and so well did the architecture assist, that it would seem they each influenced the other. However this wasn't always the case, and often the building was something purely of the imagination, with some authors even suggesting beginners should start by drawing the memory palace out in sand or on paper in the manner of a master builder so as to be able to picture it in the mind's eye.[32]

A Form of Moral Improvement

The association between memory and morality that began to be hinted at in the classical art of memory grew greatly with its new Christian focus. As a result the whole practice became far more meditative and increasingly associated with inner transformation and self improvement, which could be seen as the beginnings of what would modernly be seen as creative visualisation or auto suggestion.

Reading medieval works on memory immediately gives the sense that they viewed memory, and indeed human consciousness, in a very

[28] Hugh of St Victor *A little Book about constructing Noah's Ark* 1125.
[29] Daniel Featley, *Four Rows of Precious Stones*, 1610 - The same memory device can be found in the works of St Jerome
[30] Guglielmo Gratarolo *The Castle of Memory* 1562.
[31] Alan Lille *On the Six Wings of the Seraph* c. 1200.
[32] Regarding the works of Hugh of St Victor see Mary Carruthers and Jan M. Ziolkowski, *The Medieval Craft of Memory An Anthology of Texts and Pictures* 30.

different way to how it is now. Modernly it is accepted that what is experienced in life affects the mind and that very strong experiences can bring around a permanent change to the personality. For example, a traumatic experience can mean that a strong association is made with the cause from then on. For example, a life-threatening burn may lead to a fear of fire. Likewise the power of positive reinforcement and inspiration is largely unquestioned. This was the same in medieval times, but they took it far further. It was believed that what was remembered became part of the functioning consciousness. It's almost as if from the medieval mindset whatever was put into the mind became a part of the personality.

With a new Christian focus on the art of memory it's understandable that there would a stronger focus on virtue. It could however also be that this association between memory and moral regeneration grew due to the close association between Cicero's work on rhetoric, which had a strong focus on morality, and the *Ad Herennium*, which had a complete focus on artificial memory. These were often put together as the two books of Tullius in the high medieval period. Viewed as one work it's understandable how the art could have taken a stronger direction towards moral regeneration. Indeed reading contemporary notebooks and memory treatises written by practitioners gives the feel that for them mnemonics was a route to remembering the virtues man had before his fall from the Garden of Eden, or sometimes even developing angel like qualities. For this reason in the medieval period the art of memory was increasingly disassociated with rhetoric and more commonly viewed as part of the virtue of prudence.[33] Practiced as part of the disciplines of Christianity it flourished in monasteries. Indeed Saint Thomas Aquinas recommended the use of the memory temple as a means to meditate on the virtues and to improve one's piety. In the words of the saint himself:

'Spiritual and simple intentions slip easily from the soul

---

[33] Cicero in his *De Inventione* repeatedly lists memory as one of three parts of prudence along with intelligence and foresight.

unless they are linked with certain corporeal similitudes.'[34]

The above quote appears in almost all of the English and Scottish Christian memory manuals of the medieval period. A 'corporeal similitude' is a medieval term for an anthropomorphic image that would serve as a memory aid if placed in a specific location in the memory palace.

So how did it work?

Within the Church nothing was done thoughtlessly, and the mechanism whereby the memorisation of corporeal similitudes would cause inner transformation to the personality was well known to the educated.

St Albert described how it was thought this worked in detail. According to him a very emotional or important experience creates an imprint in the mind which forms a permanent association; the art of memory works along the same lines, but the imprint is created deliberately. By dedicated repetition it becomes an image within oneself which has its own inbuilt intention, bringing with it responses and impulses. The term he uses for this is 'estimative power', which is a philosophical term referring to the kind of intelligence an animal has whereby it can respond to situations with simple, non-verbal, or abstract, thought. So, for example, if you memorised wolf strongly it would help you remain aware of the risks of wolves and remind you to flee![35]

This philosophy is reflected in the works of many other Christian writers of the time, including St Albert's own student St Thomas Aquinas. In some works this statement is supported by a quote from Aristotle saying that 'it is impossible to think without a mental picture.'[36] Aristotle when making this point actually mentions that

[34] St. Thomas Aquinas *Summa Theologica* (Translated by The Fathers of the English Dominican Province, 1947) II, II, 49
[35] This is actually the exact example of this principle St Albertus gives in his work *De Anima*, which is a commentary on the work by Aristotle of the same name.
[36] He declares this several times in his work *On Memory and. Recollection*.

this is why the images used in mnemonics were so effective. To St Thomas this was a clear recommendation that the route to salvation was through the use of the art of memory, to ensure the image that came to mind when any subject was brought to focus, would always be a holy and virtuous one.

Thus within the Church memory and religious iconography became combined. Statues of virtues, saints, and angels were created with detailed clothing, objects, and symbolic positioning, all of which when memorised would create or strengthen a virtue or holy presence in the mind of the practitioner. This practice became the norm with stained glass windows, paintings, and manuscripts created in a 'memorable' way so as to become a lesson in virtue and piety that would stay in the mind.

The trickle down effect of all this practice was that it became a common belief that by memorising a song or a poem about a particular virtue it would change the person's way of thinking. In fact at the time it was common practice for the priest to prescribe the memorisation of set words or a prayer focused on virtue as a way to cure an ongoing problem with vice. Likewise he may instead recommend the contemplation of set scenes from stories in the Bible that would allow the mind to dwell in the correct spirit for salvation and moral improvement.

A Doorway to the Divine
During this time a new more meditative and reverent approach to the art of memory started to appear. This was partly due to the religious and moral focus of art, but also to some degree due to corrupt Latin in some of the manuscripts in possession of the masters of that day. So the advice given in the text *Ad Herennium* which stated that one should choose images that are exciting, became a injunction to 'cleave with affection to the holy images.' Likewise the statement that the place chosen for the memory palace should be remote and free of visitors, became interpreted as a commandment for mystical retreat.

Cicero and Aristotle's works were combined with a sense of religious awe and a new form of Christian practice was born. A meditative form of memory whereby one would retire in retreat and practice walking through a holy memory palace while full of feelings of religious devotion and awe. The locations and figures in them would be so detailed to cover every aspect of the teachings that one's mind would remain fully focused in every moment in a state of pure meditation.

Some mystically inclined practitioners used some very intense memory palaces. Mother Julian of Norwich recounted in her writings the use of the actual body of Christ on the cross as her memory palace, assigning a symbolic meaning to each of the five wounds, crown of thorns, and every small aspect. Often the practitioner would travel through the levels of hell, purgatory, and heaven. In hell there would be figures of devils to implant fear towards sin in each level, with symbolic figures of redemptive acts in purgatory, and angels or virtues ready to greet them in heaven. Using this sustained high level of focus with reverence and intense concentration made the art of memory a mystical experience for many practitioners. Indeed, reading the actual accounts of Dominican monks, saints and scholars of the time they can be quite breathtaking. Many felt that when using the the levels of heaven as a memory temple they slipped through momentary to the actual place. This experience was supported by biblical accounts in the Old and New Testaments describing what seemed to be the very same thing happening. More often this was described as a form of remembering the divine, as if by searching through memory the practitioner had found the only presence in his consciousness beyond all memory and thus had with great irony remembered God himself. The most famous account of this was from St Augustine who stated in *Confessions* that he had experienced oneness with God in the *'fields and spacious palaces of memory.'*[37]

With such an endorsement from one of the very early Christian saints, the art of memory continued throughout the medieval period, enduring religious upheaval. In fact, rather interestingly it would

[37] Pusey, E.B (*trans.*) *Confessions of St. Augustine: Spiritual Meditations and Divine Insights* (Watkins Publishing, 2012) VIII, 12.

seem that change often brought extra force to the art and in England and Scotland the Protestant Reformation actually increased the practice of the art of memory. It would seem that when the outer images were removed, the dedicated practitioners turned inwards and sought them inside their mind's eye.

Methods of Medieval Memory

The art of memory's heyday was during the medieval period, during which its main focus was as a form of moral training or religious practice, although it was also very much employed for practical learning purposes too. Known at the time as *artificial memory* or *the Craft of Memory* the methods and practices laid out in the classical treatises were fully applied to all areas of learning. In fact the main problem any researcher has in this area is that the memory principles became so integrated, so much a part of how things were presented and learned, that they are very rarely mentioned specifically. Combining beautifully with the symbolism and iconography of the Christian faith and the need to teach the illiterate, images put in locations in a set order became the natural way to teach and remember anything. There were several ways this art was expressed.

Corporeal Similitudes

As previously mentioned this term was coined by St Thomas Aquinas and refers to any anthropomorphic image created for memory. During the medieval period the principle of making images stand out using emotion was taken to the extreme, with the levels of hell in the memory palace not just being populated by hideous demons, but also wanton, wayward women demonstrating vices. Some of these images were made deliberately shocking, so much so, that sometimes practitioners had to be reigned in by Church authorities who were worried they were getting too interested in the sexualised images of vice, and that rather than being repulsed, they were being drawn in.

Holy and virtuous images however were encouraged and spread throughout Christendom. Take a glance at any Catholic or 'High' church to see plenty of images of virtues and vices, holding symbolic items in specific locations. Corporeal similitudes however were used to remember many different things too. Biographies of great saints, teachers, and martyrs were often recorded using statues of them holding items related to the achievements or events of their life. Likewise graces, virtues, crafts, and a whole story could be summarised in one anthropomorphic image.

The Seven Liberal Arts – Picture from the Hortus Deliciarum of Herrad of Landsberg (12th century).

The Master Builder Trope

In medieval mnemonic texts various analogies were used for the process of building a new character through the building of a memory palace. Sometimes it is through forming a string of beads on a rosary or collecting relics, but by far the most popular of these analogies was the master builder trope.[38] In this the practitioner in the process of building a memory palace was compared to a master builder. This was inspired by Paul calling the faithful Christian the 'master builder'[39] and entreating the faithful to build themselves into a living temple for God. This, and other biblical quotes using the building metaphor, became a wholesale licence for the inner construction of a memory temple to meditate upon.

The medieval practitioners of memory believed that as they did this they were actually rebuilding their inner landscape and transforming their character which in turn would lead to salvation. This was not seen as a new invention, but rather was viewed as clearly an ancient practice. Some very zealous writers even believed that Solomon was practicing the memory art. After all, Solomon's temple was said to have been created without the sound of tools, so it could only have been of the mind, not of the physical. This analogy of building the inner temple or 'raising a spiritual superstructure' was really emphasised as a memory method in the works of St Gregory the Great, Hugh of St Victor and his Scottish student, Richard of St Victor. These texts were very well read, especially in the British Isles, with the centre of influence of this tradition being Dryburgh Abbey where they printed[40] the works of St Victor's tradition and other texts inspired by similar themes.[41]

This comparison led to the art including a great deal of sacred geometry, and symbolic meaning was added to all aspects of the inner

---

[38] Carrithers, M., *The Craft of Thought: Meditation, Rhetoric, and the Making of Images, 400-1200* (Cambridge Studies in Medieval Literature 1998) 16.
[39] 1 Corinthians 3:10.
[40] Carrithers, M., *The Medieval Craft of Memory: An Anthology of Texts and Pictures* (University of Pennsylvania Press, 2003) 48.
[41] E.g. *Three Part Tabernacle, Together with a Picture* by Adam of Dryburgh *c.* 1200AD.

work. Sometimes the process of drawing plans was linked to the divine plan and often the lifting tool used by the stonemasons was seen as symbolic: just as the objects of construction are lifted with the *machina* of the builder, the faithful are lifted with the machinery of the divine, the *machina universalis*.[42] Likewise chipping and scraping away stone to shape the brick or keystone very much features as part of forming locations in the mind and thus virtues in the soul.[43]

Noah's Ark as a Memory Palace in the Work of Hugh of St Victor.

Catechisms

Almost all medieval formal learning involved a question and answer format. Sometimes these questions and answers would take a form based on the art of memory, such as asking questions in a where/what format with only small departures into detail. Sometimes the test would even be based on a picture with items laid out to trigger the memory. However, compared to other learning practices, this method of medieval education had the highest tendency to depart from the rules of the art of memory and take on a parrot learning style. Catechisms would remain the mainstay of Christian education well into the Renaissance and beyond, persisting in some churches and sects to this very day.

[42] This is very much expressed in sermon 13a by Maximus the Bishop of Turin 5AD (Catholic Online Network Library).
[43] See Hugh of St Victor's *Didacalicon* (Columbia University Press; New Ed edition, 1991) vi.4.

Emblems and Iconography

Returning once again to one of the core texts, *Ad Herennium* suggested that a picture could be used as a memory palace. This was especially useful for a largely illiterate medieval population and was expressed in various ways from painted images in churches showing the stations of the cross, to the stained glass windows put together to make them 'memorable'. Throughout Christendom icons were scattered with symbolic gestures, items, and images of places connected with biblical events and lessons. With the works of Tullius being required reading amongst the educated, and real locations being used by the religious as memory palaces, it's reasonable to suggest that even the churches themselves were being designed with these principles in mind. Of course many of these churches still remain, and visiting churches built at the time can show that they were indeed created with these exact instructions in mind with perfect levels of lighting, a quiet atmosphere, and convenient locations (very often evenly spaced apart), and often with memorable figures and images already placed there.

But it wasn't just in the Church this was practiced. It became very popular to have educational images in the form of paintings, drapes, and furniture. Even whole illustrated books full of symbolic memory images were widely circulated.[44] The most popular works of this type were those documenting different animals known as 'bestiaries'. Likewise there are some exceptional medieval paintings and tapestries that tell a story or epic tale using the art of memory and that may well have been used as entertainment.

In the late medieval period a whole new world of possibilities arrived with the invention of the printing press. A new kind of title appeared known as emblem books and these were beautifully illustrated with woodcuts. These contained moral, biblical, and sometimes historical lessons to be learned by the owner. But these were not to just be mused upon gently or used as a diversion, this was

[44] See Freeman, R., *English Emblem Books* (Chatto & Windus; New Impression Edition, 1966)

the lay mediation practice with clear instructions for *contemplatio* or *meditatio*. Sometimes the images were very simple such as a picture with a poem, but often they were full blown memory temples with the locations clearly marked in the order they should be visited. The connection with the art of memory here was very overt, with some treatises even making direct reference to it. However, with such popularity also came some variation and sometimes an actual departure from the cultivation of virtue, memory games in books for women start to appear by the start of the Renaissance and texts for men who wanted to improve their memory.

Printing and literacy both grew as the medieval period waned, but the art of memory continued with full force through the Renaissance and well into the Age of Reason, and even beyond. Something new started to appear in the emblem books, alchemical symbols and Rosicrucian figures, foreshadowing a new form of memory with more ambitious goals.

The Hermetic Art of Memory

In 1543 the Italian mnemonic Magus Giulio Camillo visited the zoo in Paris with a number of his learned friends. They were walking through the zoo when all of a sudden a great cry went up alerting visitors to an escaped lion. People began to run in panic and all of Giulio's party fled, all that was, but Giulio who remained absolutely still. Rather than run he entered into his memory palace, which took the form of a great theatre and rising through the planets settled in the room of the sun. Being thus ensconced, he took on the form of Apollo Helios, the sun god, and allowed the light to shine through him. Returning his consciousness to his bodily form, he became aware that the lion was upon him. However its claws were withdrawn and the lion seemed to only be concerned with licking Camillo, an affection attributed to his solar virtue, and so Camillo was spared from harm. Furthermore, it was reported that the lion thereafter stopped snarling and lost all aggression and became subservient to him.[45]

This story is known not only from Camillo's own account, but also from others that were there. One such description is found in the diaries of his friend Betussi[46] who gave a very similar account, but with one extra detail. He says that the only reason Camillo had to reduce to magical influence was that he was far too fat to run!

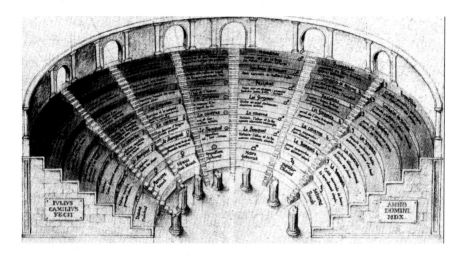

Giulio Camillo's Theatre of Memory (1511 AD).

Whatever the reason, this story is important because it perfectly described the desired effect and modus operandi of the Hermetic art of memory.

The Renaissance saw an amazing celebration of knowledge and a resurgence of interest in all things ancient, including many mystical and magical texts of the past being translated and circulated throughout Europe. Arguably the most influential of these newly discovered works were the Hermetic texts; namely the *Corpus Hermeticum* and the *Perfect Discourse*. Hermetic philosophy viewed all things as being formed of pure consciousness. The whole of existence was alive, moving, and dynamic, underpinned by a great

[45] Yates, F., *The Art of Memory* (Routledge & Kegan Paul, 1966) 133.
[46] ibid.

universal mind. It was thought that just as man forms images in the imagination, so too does the divine mind form all material things.

In the mixing pot of different philosophies of the time a love affair was in the making. To the Hermeticist the whole of the art of memory was magical. Memory, after all, was the art of making an imprint in the mind, a reflection of divine creation. A precedence could also be found in the *Hermetica* too! The *Corpus Hermeticum* starts with a meeting with the mind of god in which the protagonist Hermes was told to be silent and hold in his mind all he would wish to understand. To the practitioners of the time this was clear evidence that the memory practice was ancient, Hermetic, and original to Egypt. Besides, Hermes was a messenger god and messengers had always practiced the memory arts in ancient times as part of their duties.

The Hermeticists took hold of the art of memory and made it their own. Gone were the memory temples based on churches or biblical places. King Solomon's temple was replaced by a divine theatre of Ancient Greece complete with the gods of the planets as aids. The levels of heaven became the platonic harmony of the planetary spheres.

By the time of the Schaw Statutes quoted at the start, there were many memory experts touring Europe and teaching the art, both in the traditional classical form (for practical use and for moral self improvement) and in its latest incarnation as a Hermetic art of memory (a means of enlightenment). So in vogue were these memory experts that monarchs themselves would pay for tuition and act as patrons of this art form.

During this time there was an increase in the already significant focus on the number seven. This was partly due to the seven pillars of wisdom mentioned in the Bible, the seven liberal arts of classical education, the seven virtues, and of course the seven planets. The Hermetic texts also talked of seven builders that made the whole of the universe in the form of the planets. This gave a perfect classification system with both exciting figures (angels or gods) and interesting locations (planets) for them to stand on. To the practitioner, by forming these figures in their memory palace they were laying out their inner world as a reflection of the outer.

Implanting Divine Statues in the Soul

The beautifully captivating ancient Hermetic works not only explained this process, but also offered techniques that could aid the practitioner in this quest. These included intense forms of contemplation and imagination exercises. In addition to this, some methods involved drawing down divine influences. It was believed that each planet had the energy of consciousness and if a statue was created which was in sympathy with the one of the divine forms this consciousness would descend into the statue and bring the blessings and powers of that deity with it. To create this sympathy the practitioner needed to make sure the statue was an accurately symbolic representation and was of a substance which had resonance with the planet. So for example, to draw down Venus, the planet of love, to come take on a material form first a statue must be formed, perhaps of white sapphire or some other stone conducive to her energy. This statue must then be anointed with a oil such as rose and surrounded with symbols and objects related to her powers. Many prayers of love and of compassion must be sung and sweet incense and music played in harmony with the venereal nature. Upon reading this the practitioners of the time immediately connected the statues of Ancient Egypt to the symbolic figures in the art of memory. Corporeal similitudes were about to be replaced with divinely imbued inner statues.

The perceived similarities didn't end there. The Hermeticist compared the repeated practice of walking the memory temple with the circumambulation used to charge and bring life to statues with the presence of gods, or the repeated prayer and anointing of statues in churches. Furthermore, they speculated as to if a building or temple was repeatedly brought to mind with specific virtues or qualities then perhaps it could become like a living talisman bringing goodness into the world. For the philosophers at the time it was clear that if all things were made from thoughts manifest, then memory was the art of making thoughts become real. The prime aim of the Hermetic art of memory was from this moment onwards to bring about inner purification and deification by creating an inner temple filled with divine figures who would take on the divine energy from the world of forms and thus bring these powers to the practitioner.

Climbing the Planetary Spheres

The Hermetic teachings taught that with special training it was possible to perfect one's own mind, forming a godlike consciousness that could let go of its limitations and ascend through the seven planets back to the original divine consciousness.

Many of the Hermetic scholars were Christian and had already trained in the Christian art of memory. Not only that, but they were also well versed in a discipline which involved solitary meditation involving intense imagination. With a focus on the cultivation of virtues and the creation of highly symbolic figures, the medieval art of memory often used the levels of hell, purgatory, and heaven as a memory palace and forms of angels representing the penances, lessons, and virtues they needed to remember to reach each level. The Christian imagery was blended and adjusted to fit with the planetary and kabbalistic spheres of the Hermeticists.

A simple memory palace based on the elements from Giordano Bruno's book *Ars Memoriae* (1585).

The Hermeticists took the Christian practice of using the levels of heaven as a memory palace literally. To them Paul's assent to heaven in the New Testament made it quite clear that to do so was most certainly possible.[47] The cultivation of virtue continued but as very important part of the Hermetic process of self purification needed to allow the practitioner to rise through the heavens,[48] which to them must of course be the rising through the planetary planes. Unlike in the Christian art of memory where practitioners memorised virtues in order to live a noble life and thus enter heaven upon their death, to the Hermeticist this process was not symbolic or a rehearsal, but rather a road map where they, like Enoch and Hermes, were going to literally walk through the levels of heaven.

The Hermetic texts described the ascent taking place in various ways, either through the spheres or through the decans or the signs of the zodiac. For this reason these were the most popular memory palaces for the Hermeticist to make. There are many examples of this practice, normally based on the figures of the planets or associated gods as per Camillo's theatre, or the images of the decans from the *Picatrix*. One very influential example of this was the *Hieroglyphic Monad* by the English Elizabethan Dr John Dee, which was a system of planetary, magical, alchemical contemplation based on a sacred symbol. This sacred symbol of the *Hieroglyphic Monad* was formed from various traditional symbols for the planets combined. The practitioner would commit each of these to the 'creative memory' while combining them to form the monad inside themselves, thus connecting with the magical powers of each planet and bringing about a magical transformation inside.

The newly formed Hermetic art was divided by its practitioners into two categories, 'the Square' and 'the Curved'. The square art tended to use square images or buildings as its basis. Its focus was on the balancing and perfecting of the four elements in man. During this stage the Hermetic mnemonic magus would transform all his vices to virtues and bring the humors into balance. The second stage received far more focus and would involve a far more complicated memory palace, normally based on some diagram of the universe at large - the planes of existence, the planets, the signs of the zodiac,

---

[47] 2 Corinthians 12:2
[48] *The Corpus Hermeticum* 5:25

the 32 decans. This art had a focus on attracting divine powers into the the mind of the practitioner and in time stepping forth into the other realms.

Combinatory Wheels

Some examples of Hermetic memory wheels from Giordano Bruno, *Ars Memoriae*, 1582

The Hermetic practitioners, especially Giordano Bruno and Robert Fludd, were very influenced by the Lullian arts. Several centuries earlier, inspired by Jewish kabbalistic meditations on Hebrew letters, the Christian mystic Raymond Llull had a vision of universal truth found in the three monotheistic faiths. Combining religious and philosophical attributes he made a mechanical device which he believed showed that Christian doctrine could be deduced from set ideas. A system whereby any question could be answered by the contemplation of specific divine qualities and principles. To do this he created wheels which were subdivided into letters representing the different qualities. Two or more of these circles were used together so that with rotation different qualities could be combined for contemplation. This Lullian art was before its time.[49] When the Renaissance came to full force the dream of a pansophic system whereby all questions could be answered became a focus of all learned men, especially those who devoted themselves to the alchemical or esoteric arts, and Llull's art inspired a new art of

---

[49] Blessed Ramon Llull (*c.*1232 - *c.*1316) wrote most of his works in the thirteenth century.

memory. In addition to being a tool for ecstatic contemplation, memory wheels became a very efficient way of forming memory systems. Three wheels together each one represented a person, object, and action, which created a very powerful system especially for the memorisation of words.

Contractions

Reading the works of Dee, Dicsone, and Bruno it becomes clear that to the Hermeticist the art of memory involved patterning the inner world to match the universe of the outer world. As the inner and outer became one, it was believed that the practitioner would start to have some direct experience of the divine. Dee called this experience 'the ecstasy of union,' but only Bruno took the time to classify these states in detail.[50] These contractions, as he called them, were seen as clear signs of the alchemical rebirth taking place in the practitioner and read very much like the states of Samadhi described in Indian yogic texts.

Masonic Mnemonics?

Having explored the three main schools of the art of memory it is now time to compare them with the memory methods used within Freemasonry with a goal to establish which art of memory Schaw was most likely referring to in his Statutes. Knowing this influence on the formation of the Craft can also offer a valuable insight into the original aims of Masonry. Freemasonry has a very large, rich, and varied tradition with many influences, which has led to many branches and practices across the world. For the sake of clarity, this paper is focused on examining what is termed 'Craft Masonry' or 'Blue Lodge'. That would be the three earliest recorded Masonic degrees namely that of the Entered Apprentice, the Fellow Craft, and the Master Mason, which were clearly evolved and elaborated from

[50] Bruno, G., *Thirty Seals & The Seal Of Seals* (Online English translation by Scott Gosnell, 2016)

the practices that Schaw was referring to. The goal here is purely to look at Masonic beliefs, methods and practices in terms of Masonic memory traditions, rather than any philosophical or linguistic content of the ritual.

Masonic Attitudes Towards Memory

Memory is very important in Freemasonry. Lengthy Masonic rituals are memorised word for word to be performed without the slightest variation or error. Ritual teaching and testing is still practiced in the same way Schaw mentions, Freemasons learn the symbols in the temple and the precise positioning of the ornaments, furniture, and officers of the lodge room. They make sure that everything is precisely positioned, keep to ceremonial ritual procedures, and observe various Masonic offices, ranks, and regalia meticulously. In Freemasonry memory is a very good thing to be respected and cultivated.

The Purpose of Masonic Memorisation

The classical art of rhetoric was very focused on eloquence and although Freemasons value this it's not the goal of their practice. Some Masons, with Hermetic or mystical leanings, seek divine union and see Freemasonry as part of this goal, but the truth is Masonic ritual never states this as a goal and there is little more than a faint hint of it in any of the early Masonic documents. Considering these were written at a time when many practitioners were very overt about their Hermetic goals, this silence would be surprising.

In truth the goal of Masonic ritual is very clear, Freemasonry is focused on the cultivation of virtue. This has been the focus and remains the focus of the Craft to this day, as shown by Grand Lodges using slogans like 'making good men better'[51] and even Masonic

---

[51] The earliest occurrence I can find of this is by Roscoe Pound in *Masonic Addresses and Writings of Roscoe Pound* (New York: Macoy, 1953) 20–21. A contemporary example is found on https://www.ugle.org.uk/about-freemasonry

ritual itself defining Freemasonry as 'a peculiar system of morality, veiled in allegory and illustrated by symbols.'[52]

So, how do Freemasons believe that Freemasonry brings around this moral regeneration? By the memorisation of ritual and the contemplation of the lessons it contains. Indeed anyone who reads Masonic ritual from the earliest exposés to the modern day ritual books will see how the ritual text clearly and repeatedly self defines as a form of moral training. With the candidate learning the 'principles of moral truth'[53] and to 'subdue his passions and perfect his character.'[54] Indeed the connection between memorisation and inner morality is so strong in Freemasonry that it is rarely questioned. It seems those who do invest in the hours need to memorise the ritual do indeed find themselves expressing the lessons they teach in their daily life. This connection between ritual learning and moral excellence is a belief that in modern society Freemasons alone seem to hold. This belief that stands at the very centre of the Masonic sense of self also stands out as clear relic of the medieval Christian art of memory.

The Lodge as a Memory Palace

When looking at the layout of a Masonic lodge, from modern times to its earliest incarnation, it does indeed seem to meet all the criteria for a memory palace exactly as described in *Ad Herennium*:

> 'The artificial memory includes backgrounds and images. By backgrounds I mean such scenes as are naturally or artificially set off on a small scale, complete and conspicuous, so that we can grasp and embrace them easily by the natural memory - for example, a house, an intercolumnar space, a recess, an arch, or the like.'[55]

---

[52] This phrase appears in the vast majority of English Masonic ritual books as part of the the questions leading to the Second Degree (Fellow Craft).

[53] A statement as to the purpose of the 'Entered Apprentice Degree' is made in 'The Exhortation of the Master Mason' from English Masonic ritual.

[54] A common phrase in American Masonic ritual.

[55] Loeb Classical Library, *Ad Herennium* (Loeb Classical Library, 1954) 209.

Masonic tradition is fastidiously focused on the location of objects with very strict rules and practices as to the layout of the lodge. In fact it matches all the rules to the letter, including the correct number of locations with clear and regular spacing.

Looking at the earliest of the Masonic catechisms it can be seen that an imaginary lodge has always been part of Masonic practice[56] and that a candidate would be expected to remember the details of the lodge as part of their test, something that continues to be important up to this day. The lodge may vary somewhat, but there are common themes that persist including the Master of the Lodge and his two Wardens, a chequered carpet, two pillars representing the pillars and stonemasons tools given symbolic importance.

Although a direct reference in Masonic text to the lodge being a memory palace has yet to be found, in an early Masonic exposé it is referred to as the 'Grand Building termed a Mosaic Palace.'[57] This is in reference to a practice described in early Masonic exposés and verified in the minutes of early lodges.[58] It would seem that it was the Tyler's duty to draw on the floor of the tavern using chalk and charcoal a design representing a building. This would be seen both as the form of the lodge and the ground plan of King Solomon's temple. Filled with various Masonic emblems, these were all carefully drawn in black and white. These Masonic symbols and

[56] See Professor David Stephenson *The Origins of Freemasonry* (Cambridge University Press, 1990) for a conclusive case that memorisation of the layout or drawing of the lodge in detail was required of members since earliest times.
[57] *Jachin and Boaz* (London, W. Nicoll 1762)
[58] The "Tyler's fee" in different lodges varied from 6d. to 2/6. In the Old Dundee Lodge the amount was originally 6d. It was raised to 1/6 in 1771 and to 2.6 in 1795. It was 2/6 in the Lodge of Felicity in 1738 and also in the Old Kings Arms Lodge, No. 28, in 1752. Thus in the minutes of the Old Dundee Lodge, No. 18, one of the oldest London Lodges, we have the following: '1795, August 13th, paid Bro. Geo. Mills, (Tyler) for "framing and forming the Lodge"' 2/6'; '1799, August 8th. paid Bro. Mills (Tyler) for "forming 6 Lodge," 15/,' and in the minutes of the Grenadiers Lodge, '1763, November 14th, "Agreed by this Lodge that Bro. Lister be a free member for drawing the Lodges except no Making or Raising in the quarter then he is under obligation to pay."' According to the minutes of the Shakespeare Lodge, a whiting box and penknife were bought on Jan. 26th, 1774, for the sum of £1. See Norman B. Spencer, *Drawing the Lodge* (Selected papers, Vol.1 United Masters Lodge No. 167, Auckland 1929)

emblems were then carefully explained to the candidate to impress on the candidate's memory the great lessons and symbolism of Freemasonry. After their description had been completed the candidate was handed a mop and pail of water and compelled to wash away the depictions.[59] It is also written that the layout of the lodge was drawn out on the floor of a tavern, or formed using red ribbon pinned on the floor of the lodge, the purpose being to aid the imagination of the brethren present. It also seems that often tiles or metal plates with symbols on them[60] were placed about the floor in different locations to form part of the symbolic temple. As previously mentioned, this process of drawing out a memory palace on the floor to aid the imagination is something that appears in some medieval memory manuals also.

Most importantly the Masonic lodge from the earliest times has been a representation of King Solomon's Temple. This of course immediately points to the Christian art of memory which, unlike the classical art which encouraged the practitioner to choose locations they visited all the time, or the Hermetic art which favoured the use of celestial objects or constellations, unsurprisingly the Christian art of memory favoured memory palaces based on locations from the Bible that were thought to hold a lesson.

Memorisation by Catechism

Works which were designed for memorisation took the form of interlocution in the classical and Hermetic (in imitation of the classical) memory arts. Freemasonry however, like the Christian art, has always used catechisms. Indeed there are examples of this in the earliest Masonic fragments from not long after Schaw's time. More than just a way of testing membership the similarity of this form of memory work with that of the church didn't escape Masons indeed one Masonic exposé even stated that 'every Mason sitting around a

---

[59] See *The Three Distinct Knocks* (1760)
[60] See Terry Haunch *Tracing Boards, Their Development & Their Designers* (QC Correspondence Circle Ltd 2004) for many detailed examples.

table answer in term in the manner as boy at church saying Catechism."[61]

Corporeal Similitudes

Figures symbolic of virtue are powerfully and prominently featured in Masonic traditions. This can be seen in early and current Masonic Tracing Boards where the seven virtues, and sometimes the liberal arts, are depicted as angelic figures. On some of the older descriptions whole figures of ideal Masons can be seen made up of their tools, each having a symbolic meaning.

In addition to this, lodge officers could be seen as corporeal similitudes themselves, being figures representing virtues. In Masonic lodges the principal officers (the Master and two Wardens) are positioned at pedestals. Next to each of these is a pillar with symbolic meaning: one corinthian meaning wisdom, one doric meaning strength, and one composite meaning beauty.[62] Early Masonic exposés include reference to the Master and the Wardens as actually representing these pillars and are intended to embody their symbolic qualities.[63] The pedestals before them also have items representing moral lessons. Although these vary, they are usually the square, compasses, and plumb rule. In addition to these other symbols are often placed on the pedestals in the form of a rough and smooth ashlar and a builder's lewis. The Wardens also each have one symbolic miniature column, each representing a pillar of King Solomon's Temple, one topped with a celestial globe and the other a terrestrial. Within Freemasonry these rules are strictly applied, the Wardens must never be out of their seat and the symbolic items that they possess must never be misplaced or moved. Although the earliest records that show this level of detail in a lodge are seventeenth century Masonic exposés, the whole layout and structure is exactly that of a medieval

---

[61] *Jachin and Boaz* (London, W. Nicoll 1762) 44.
[62] This may be from *De Architectura* by Vitruvius, where he says that any building must have three attributes: strength, usefulness, and beauty.
[63] See *The English Masonic Exposures of 1760-1769: With full transcripts of Three distinct knocks, 1760, Jachin and Boaz, 1762, Shibboleth, 1765* (Lewis Masonic, 1986).

symbolic representation or corporeal similitude with a central figures being in a set location with symbolic clothing and objects. Furthermore, it is known from very early ritual fragments that the roles of Master and two Wardens existed in the lodge around the time of the Schaw statutes.[64]

This whole setup is a perfect example of the medieval craft of memory: a symbolic figure, in a set location, with a detailed array of items that have deep meaning is a mainstay of medieval memory work.

A Mnemonic Routine and Locations

As previously mentioned, the mnemonic practice of a memory palace followed a set route visiting specific locations in order. Comparing this to Masonic ritual is extremely easy since it involves doing just this! The early Masonic exposés and modern ritual books alike show repeated visiting of specific locations in a set order, never doubling back, with repeated observation of symbols at each location and with triggered sections of symbol associated speeches and passwords. These circumambulations are a template of Mnemonic practice and within the context of a symbolic building can leave no doubt that Masonic ritual was heavily influenced by the practice of the art of memory.

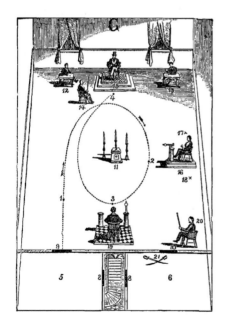

An illustration showing the route taken by the candidate through the lodge from Duncan's *Masonic Ritual and Monitor* (1866).

[64] Edinburgh Register House Manuscript, 1696.

An example of a traditional memory pilgrimage

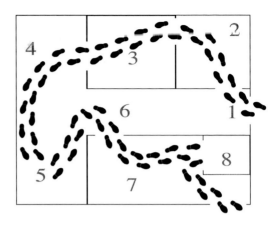

Use Of Emblems for Contemplation

In Freemasonry there is a tradition whereby each of the three Craft rituals have a painting which summarises the lessons of the degree in pictorial form. These are now commonly known as tracing boards and are accompanied by a traditional speech which moralises on each symbol within the painting. Modernly Freemasons tend to view these as objects of contemplation rather than memory aids, although those learning the sections of ritual relevant to these illustrations certainly find them so.

What Freemasons now call tracing boards may have started from the previously mentioned tradition of drawing the lodge whereby some of the depicted symbols started to be added to tiles or sections of cloth that were placed in specific locations. It would seem natural that as Masonry grew ways would be found to move towards more permanent depictions that could be simply brought out, rather than repeatedly redrawing again and again. As works started to be published on the subject these very same symbols and depictions appeared where they were rightly named emblems or memory aides.[65] Nowadays, at least in England, tracing boards are standardised and tend to be limited specifically to a few degrees and not used in all countries. If one examines the symbolism used on these works they

---

[65] One example of this would be *True Masonic Chart or Hieroglyphic Monitor* (1819).

are almost always biblical and follow the rules of the art of memory. There is a distinct preponderance to the use of corporal similitudes, both in the forms of officers in the lodge, but also in depictions of virtues. Looking at the use of Masonic tracing boards whereby each symbol is moralised upon in a set order, the similarities to the medieval and Renaissance practice of emblem books is very clear to see. There are also many works whereby each symbol works as a mnemonic trigger for a set memorised section of text. Therefore it seems fair to conclude that the evolution of tracing boards and their predecessor the floor cloth were very much influenced by the practice of contemplation on emblems. Once again the practices of Freemasonry involve the maintenance of mnemonic practices.

The Building Trope
Freemasonry is a clear expression of the building trope applied to a memory art with biblically focused memory temples and lessons. The exact same analogies of building an inner temple, or unfolding an inner superstructure, as used in Freemasonry are as prominently and powerfully featured in medieval memory manuals. Freemasonry even features the smoothing of the ashlar analogy (symbolised by rough and smooth ashlars in a Masonic lodge) as used by Hugh of St Victor and the memory masters that followed him. Perhaps the craft of memory and the craft of stonemasons were naturally united in Freemasonry.

Conclusion

The memory methods of Masonry stand out as a direct reflection of the Christian art of memory. Indeed with a focus on the seven virtues and liberal arts, the use of catechisms, Masonic orthopraxis could be straight out of a monastic mnemotechnic manual. It's probable however that the influence of the Christian art of memory upon Freemasonry was endemic rather than specific. Moral improvement and the art of memory were one and the same to the medieval mind. So, if the medieval stonemasons guilds sought to include some form of moral improvement as part of their membership, it would be very natural to include the art of memory as taught in the churches, monasteries, and convents they built in their entering rituals and ongoing training.

Indeed, with a craft so closely linked to the Church as stonemasonry, and with the craft of memory within the Church being focused on a building analogy, it would seem highly likely that the memory training of operative masons at the time would be more intensively focused on the creation of an inner superstructure than any other organisation, albeit in a very gentle form compared to the more focused and spiritual practitioners within the churches for which they worked. Of course with the Reformation and subsequent religious upheaval in the British Isles, combined with the gradual dechristianisation of Freemasonry, it's understandable how this connection to medieval Christianity could become less apparent to many who study the Craft from a modern perspective. Especially when considering that in the modern day few societies use entering ceremonies as standard and, with biblical knowledge being uncommon, the association between morality and memory has been lost and with it the association between Freemasonry and the art of memory forgotten.

However, it may well be that this is about to change. Studies into the medieval memory arts are once again taking place and new translations of Latin and Old English memory manuals appearing all the time. I believe that with each new work appearing the connection between the craft of memory and the craft of freemasonry is going be become increasingly clear. It could be that soon Freemasonry will remember its very own origins.

There is no doubt that Freemasonry has had many influences and evolutions. It's clear that the ritual and mindset of its practitioners have taken on influences from the Renaissance including those from Hermetic and Rosicrucian traditions. More research is of course needed to establish any definite connection, but this analysis is certainly suggestive of a medieval origin of Masonic tradition, mentality, and ritual practice.